I0852097

DISCARDED

LAKE OSWEGO JR. HIGH SCHOOL
2500 SW COUNTRY CLUB RD
LAKE OSWEGO, OR 97034
503-534-2335

AFRICAN ELEPHANTS
Giants of the Land

DOROTHY HINSHAW PATENT

Photographs by

ORIA DOUGLAS-HAMILTON

Holiday House / New York

UPLANDS ELEMENTARY
LAKE OSWEGO, OR

599
Pa

Text copyright © 1991 by Dorothy Hinshaw Patent
Photographs copyright © 1991 by Oria Douglas-Hamilton
All rights reserved
Printed in the United States of America
First Edition

Library of Congress Cataloging-in-Publication Data
Patent, Dorothy Hinshaw.
African elephants : giants of the land / by Dorothy Hinshaw Patent;
photographs by Oria Douglas-Hamilton.
p.   cm.
Includes index.
Summary: Describes the physical characteristics, behavior,
feeding, family life, and habitat of the African elephant.
ISBN 0-8234-0911-2
1. African elephant—Juvenile literature. [1. African elephant.
2. Elephants.] I. Douglas-Hamilton, Oria, ill. II. Title.
QL737.P98P385 1991   91-55028   CIP   AC
599.6′1′096—dc20

12770

Contents

1 Giants of the Land   5

2 Elephant Families   16

3 Mating and Birth   24

4 African Architects   30

5 Life in Africa Today   34

Index   40

CHAPTER ONE

Giants of the Land

No other animal looks quite like an elephant, with its long trunk, big ears, and thick legs. The African elephant (*Loxodonta africana*) is the largest land animal on the earth today. Only some whales, which spend their whole lives in the water, are bigger than elephants. A male African elephant can be as tall as a one-story house and weigh 12,000 to 16,500 pounds (5,450 to 7,500 kilograms). Females are much smaller—an average one is about the size of a small house trailer and weighs half as much as a male. When an elephant calf is born, it looks tiny compared to the big adults around it. But it is already 3 feet (about 1 meter) tall and weighs more than 200 pounds (90 kilograms). By the time it is nine months old, it will weigh 750 pounds (340 kilograms), as much as four adult men.

African elephants.

The African elephant's only living relative is the Asiatic elephant (*Elephas maximus*). It's easy to tell the two kinds apart. African elephants have huge ears the shape of the African continent. Their foreheads are sloped. Their backs arch up at the rear and curve down in the middle. The ears of Asian elephants are about half the size of African ones. They have bumps on their foreheads, and their backs round upward in the middle.

Tusks are important elephant tools.

Most male Asiatic elephants have tusks, while females lack them. But the majority of female African elephants as well as males are tusked. A tusk can grow as long as 13 feet (3.25 meters) and weigh 200 pounds (90 kilograms). The tusk is actually a huge tooth. Elephants use their tusks as tools for many purposes, like stripping off bark and pulling down branches to eat. Tusks are also useful in pulling up roots for food. Male elephants use their tusks in battle, too.

A typical savanna elephant.

There are actually two different kinds of African elephants. The savanna elephant (*Loxodonta africana africana*) is the largest kind. Its tusks curve forward. It lives mostly out on the open grassslands, called savannas, where scattered trees provide some shade. The savannas also have bushes and small trees, as well as swampy areas.

The forest elephant (*Loxodonta africana cyclotis*) is not as big as the savanna elephant. Its ears are smaller for its size, and its back humps up in the middle instead of arching downward. Its tusks are long and thin, point downward, and have hard, pinkish ivory.

The division between the two types of African elephant isn't always clear. Where forests meet savannas, the two types interbreed. And the elephants living in some forests appear to be the savanna type. There may be still another kind of elephant, a small pygmy. But scientists have yet to find this animal, which is said to inhabit the very dense rain forests where people rarely go.

Being an Elephant

Every part of the elephant's body has an important use. In addition to tusks, an elephant has very large teeth. Only four teeth are used at one time. The coarse food elephants eat wears their teeth down quickly. But new teeth come in behind the old ones, pushing them out when they become too worn. Elephants go through six sets of teeth during their lifetimes.

The elephant's 1-inch (2.5-centimeter) thick, wrinkled skin protects the animal from thorns and broken branches in the forest. The skin is brownish gray. But since elephants wallow in mud and blow dust over their bodies, they usually become the color of the earth where they live. The scrawny-looking elephant tail is useful, too. It has a tuft of coarse hairs up to 30 inches (75 centimeters) long on the end that makes it a good flyswatter.

The elephant's big ears are used for cooling off in hot weather. The ears have many blood vessels. Some of the vessels are ¾ inch (1.9 centimeters) in diameter. When an elephant is hot, it waves its ears back and forth. The air passing behind the ears helps cool the blood as it moves through the ear vessels. The blood can cool down as much as 3.6°F (2°C) before it goes back into the head.

Young elephants as well as adults can flap their ears.

Elephants raise their trunks to sniff the air.

The Amazing Trunk

The elephant's most useful tool is its trunk. No other animal has anything like it. The trunk is made up of the animal's nose combined with its upper lip. The trunk can weigh 300 pounds (136 kilograms). It has thousands of muscles that allow it to bend in all directions.

The nostrils are at the end of the trunk. Elephants can swim in very deep water with just the tips of their trunks sticking out. That way, they can breathe without raising their heads. Elephants have a good sense of smell. An elephant can point its trunk in just the right direction to catch a faint scent coming from as far as 5 miles (8 kilometers) away. It can also brush its trunk along the ground to pick up odors.

Elephants greeting one another with their trunks.

The trunk has other uses, too. An elephant can wrap its trunk around a branch to rip it from a bush. It is even strong enough to bend and break an entire small tree. But the trunk can also work delicately. At its tip are two fingerlike bumps that can grasp objects as small as a single leaf from a tree.

Elephants also use their trunks for drinking. A thirsty elephant sticks its trunk into the water and sucks up as much as 2½ gallons (about 10 liters) of water at a time. Then it places the end of its trunk into its mouth and drinks. When elephants bathe, they use the trunk to throw water over their backs.

Elephants also greet one another with their trunks, wrapping them together, touching each other's mouths, and brushing the trunks over each other's backs. A mother elephant uses a gentle touch with her trunk to reassure her calf or to get her baby's attention.

Elephants can cover ground quickly and even run as fast as 24 miles (38 kilometers) an hour.

Getting Around

Elephants have very thick, strong legs to carry their great weight. Each elephant foot has five toes, just like ours. Every toe on the front feet and three toes on each hind foot have thick nails at their tips. The bottom of each foot, behind the toes, has a dense protective pad. The pads are flexible, allowing the elephant to walk over stones comfortably. The pads also cushion the sound of the animal's steps so that it can move quietly despite its large size.

Feeding an Elephant

An adult elephant needs to eat more than 300 pounds (140 kilograms) of food every day. Elephants feed on a great variety of plants. Most of their diet is grass, but they also eat the leaves, bark, and fruit of many kinds of bushes and trees.

Elephants need lots of water and sometimes must travel many miles to get it. They can live for as long as four days without water. But when they find it, they really tank up. On the average, an elephant drinks around 40 gallons (150 liters) of water a day.

CHAPTER TWO

Elephant Families

Like humans, elephants live in families, but they are different from ours. A typical elephant family has from six to twelve animals. The members are adult females and their calves of various ages.

Elephants grow up slowly, like humans. A calf usually nurses from its mother for two to four years, even though it starts eating grass and other food when it is a few months old. Older calves stay near their mothers and look to them for guidance for many years. Male elephants leave their families after they reach ten years of age, but the females stay together their entire lives. For this reason, all of the animals in a band are usually closely related—sisters, daughters, and their young of various ages.

Some members of an elephant family.

Elephants on the move stay tightly bound together.

Elephants live to be 60 or 70 years old, and the oldest, wisest female in the family is its leader. She knows best where to find food and water and how to avoid enemies. It may seem strange that an animal as big as an elephant could have enemies, but it's true. Lions can kill young elephant calves. The older elephants protect the small calves if lions are around. Native tribesmen called Masai travel across the African plains with their cattle. If grass is scarce, sometimes they throw spears at elephants to protect the grass for their cattle.

When an elephant family is on the move, the animals stay quite tightly bunched together. When they are feeding or drinking, they spread out more. But the young calves stay within a few feet of their mothers, and the older calves are not much farther away.

Related Families

In a particular area, the different elephant families know one another. Scientists who have spent years studying African elephants believe that families friendly to one another are related. Perhaps their leaders are sisters. Scientists call the families that have these special relationships "kin groups" or "bond groups." There may be four or more families in one bond group.

When two families in a bond group meet, they greet one another with noisy enthusiasm. They rumble and trumpet and touch with their trunks. The families may join for a while and feed or drink together. They may gather in a tight group to rest, leaning on each other.

Two elephant families by the waterside.

Families have ways of communicating even when separated by two or three miles. For years, scientists were puzzled to see elephants that were busy feeding or involved in other activities suddenly freeze in position with their ears spread out. Recently, researchers have discovered that elephants can produce low-frequency sounds that humans can't hear. When all of the elephants in a group freeze, they are apparently listening to sounds made by other elephants out of sight.

Families in the same bond groups probably use these sounds to keep in touch. When two such families are approaching each other and getting closer, they also release a liquid from the temporal glands on the sides of their faces. The scent from the liquid is spread on the wind by the flapping of the animal's ears and most likely helps the families find one another.

This elephant is listening to low-frequency elephant sounds.

Two young males sparring.

Life of the Males

The young male elephants that leave their families live alone or together in their own all-male groups. After they leave, young males still remain close to their families. But gradually they spend more time with other males.

Male elephants may be old enough to mate at the age of twelve. But they don't usually show much interest in females until they are quite a bit older. Males often spar, practicing the fighting methods they will need later on when they compete for mates. They move toward each other, entwining their trunks or placing them in one another's mouth. Then they push their heads together, shoving and locking tusks.

These friendly matches don't become serious fights.

When fights do occur, they begin differently from a sparring match. Two bulls come toward each other with their heads high and their ears fanned out. Instead of coming together and touching with their trunks, the males maneuver for position and then rush together with all of the power of their huge bodies behind the lunge. They lock their tusks and try to twist each other off balance. The force of the fighting is sometimes great enough to break off a tusk. Fights can be exhausting, lasting as long as eight hours. Very rarely, when one animal loses its balance and falls, the other uses its tusks to stab the fallen animal in the head, killing it.

Two male elephants fighting.

CHAPTER THREE

Mating and Birth

A male elephant usually begins to show interest in females when he is in his early twenties. But the males that are successful in mating are the really big ones in the prime of life. Around the age of thirty, a male elephant enters a new phase. For two or three months each year, he goes into a special condition called *musth* (pronounced "must"). When a male elephant is in musth, he is more likely to fight with other males and is on the lookout for females that are ready to mate.

A male in musth leaves the male group and is on his own. He carries his head high and walks with long, ground-covering strides. His temporal glands stream with strong-smelling fluid. His ears flap in a special way, probably to spread the odor from the glands into the air and to pick up female sounds. He also calls out with his own unique low-frequency call that lets other elephants know that he is in musth and in a mood to fight or mate.

A musth male.

A newborn elephant with its mother.

Elephant pregnancy lasts for about 22 months, and the mother nurses her calf for another two years before she is ready to mate again. Therefore, she mates only about once every four years, unless her calf dies young. She is in mating condition for only a few days.

Females that are ready to mate have their own ways of letting males know where they are. They send out low-frequency sounds that are different from the ones males use. Scientists studying these interesting noises have broadcast recorded female sounds from loudspeakers. Males come form all around, attracted to the sound.

Mating

When a female is ready to mate, many males may find her. But she seems to be able to choose her mate, for she can run fast enough to get away from a smaller male if she wants to.

When the right musth male comes along, the pair spends several days together. Nine times out of ten, a female will choose a big musth male for mating. He will chase other males away during the three or four days that she is ready to mate.

After remaining with one female for a few days, the male leaves to find new mates, and the female resumes normal life.

Birth

Few people have seen wild elephants give birth. When an elephant is born, its has some thin, wavy red or black hair, especially on its forehead. It's hard for the newborn to position its legs under its body, but getting on its feet as soon as possible is vital to a wild baby. It must be able to gain nourishment from its mother's milk, and it needs to be able to walk to keep up with the family in its travels. The mother helps her baby to stand by using her trunk and tusks to lift it to its feet.

Once it gets up, the young elephant searches with its trunk for its mother's nipples. She has two breasts between her front legs. To nurse, the baby elephant rolls its trunk back over its head so that it can take the nipple into its mouth.

The other elephants in the family are very interested in the new youngster, and the young teenage females help the mother take care of it. An elephant mother almost always has just one baby; twins are very rare.

A mother elephant, showing one of her breasts.

CHAPTER FOUR

African Architects

The African elephant is a powerful force in shaping its own environment. Much of the savanna is open grassland mixed in with woodlands. By using its trunk and tusks to remove large plants that shade the ground, the elephant opens up sunny patches. Unless there is a drought, new plants have no trouble taking advantage of the sunlight and filling in the spaces created by elephants' feeding.

A great variety of plants grow in such areas, and they in turn attract many animals that feed on them. Zebras, gazelles, and wildebeest graze on the open grasslands. Bushbucks and giraffes browse on the new shoots and leaves of bushes and trees. Monkeys and baboons eat a variety of plants. All of these plant eaters attract predators such as cheetahs and lions, adding further to the variety of animals.

Elephants on the savanna.

Forest Elephants

The smaller forest elephant spends most of its time in the tropical rain forests, where there is more rainfall than on the savannas. These animals influence their environment just as much as the savanna elephants do. When forest elephants feed, they pull down trees, making openings in the forest. Sun-loving plants can grow there, and large animals like gorillas and forest buffalo can make their way and find food as well.

Without elephants to open up the forests, trees and bushes take over rapidly. They shade the ground, making it difficult for other plants to get a foothold. Very few hoofed animals can live in such dark forests with so few varieties of plant life. Only creatures that can get through the dense growth, like squirrels and small monkeys, can survive.

Finding Water

When drought comes, elephants use their great strength and their knowledge of their home areas to find water. The older elephants know where water flows under the surface of the ground. They dig down into the earth, using their tusks and forefeet, until they reach the water, creating open wells.

Elephants can dig in the ground and find water.

Many other creatures are attracted to the elephants' wells. Sometimes such spots are the only source of water for miles around. Without elephants to dig down to the water, many other animals would die when drought hits the savannas.

CHAPTER FIVE

Life in Africa Today

As recently as the 1930s, millions of elephants roamed the rich African plains and forests. Now there are fewer than 650,000 left. This is because the human population of Africa has increased very rapidly during the past fifty years, and people have moved onto land where wild animals once roamed. Because elephants are so large and eat so much, they need lots of land. When farms are close to where elephants live, the elephants may raid the crops, angering the farmers.

Also, people have removed trees from the land, using them to build homes and to fuel their cooking fires. When trees are cut down, less rain falls, and drought can result. The Sahara Desert in northern Africa has been growing fast, spreading farther and farther south as people cut down more trees.

As less and less land has been available for elephants be-

The sad remains of elephants killed for their tusks.

cause of drought and increased human population, the number of elephants has declined.

The worst enemy of elephants today is the ivory trader. The strong and useful tusks of the elephant now threaten its existence. Many people want to buy things made from ivory, making ivory valuable. Even in parks where elephants are protected, poachers (illegal hunters) sneak in and kill them, taking their tusks and leaving their bodies to rot.

Effects of Poaching

Like human children, young elephants must learn most of what they know about the world from the adults around them. It takes years for them to learn where the best food is and where to find water during a drought. The elephant families really count on the knowledge of their wise leaders. When the older animals in a family are killed by ivory hunters, the young ones have a very difficult time making their way in the world. They become unsure of themselves and frightened. They are much more likely to die of thirst or hunger during a drought than are elephants led by a wise, experienced leader.

The largest males are the most prized by poachers because they have the biggest tusks. In most parts of Africa, all of the big, experienced males have been slaughtered. Even in areas where there are still females of breeding age, there may be no musth males left to mate successfully. This makes it very difficult for the elephant population to recover, even when poaching has been controlled.

People must stop buying ivory so that elephants can survive in peace.

Elephants are an important reason tourists visit Africa.

Saving Elephants

Elephants are the oldest living land mammals. They are intelligent and adaptable, but they have no way to defend themselves against the powerful guns of the poachers. Because so many elephants are killed to supply the ivory traders, concerned nations of the world have joined to ban the selling of ivory. But saving the African elephant won't be easy as long as people in wealthy nations crave ivory, and some illegal trade still goes on. Fortunately, more and more people today realize that if they buy ivory trinkets, elephants will continue to die.

We need to do everything we can to help these magnificent animals survive. It is the people who can afford to buy ivory and who choose to do so who really threaten the survival of elephants. By being responsible world citizens who consider the effects of our actions on the natural world, we can help elephants and other wild things to survive on our crowded planet.

Each pair of tusks means a dead elephant.

Index

(Numbers in *italics* refer to pages with illustrations.)

Asiatic elephant, 6, 7

babies, (*see* calves)
birth, 28
bond group, *18*, 19, 20

calves, 16, *26*, 28, *29*, 36
cooling, 10

drinking, 13, 15
drought, 32, *33*, 34–36

ears, 6, 10, 20, 24
Elephas maximus, 6

families, 16, *17*, 36
feet, 14
fighting, *22–23*, 24
food, 15
forest elephants, 32

hearing, 20, *21*

ivory trade, 35, 36, *37–39*

kin groups, *19*

Loxodonta africana, 5, 8
Loxodonta africana africana, 8
Loxodonta africana cyclotis, 8

Masai, 18
mating, 24, 26, 27
musth, 24, *25*, 27, 36

newborns, (*see* calves)
nursing, 28, *29*

poaching, 35, 36
pregnancy, 26

Sahara Desert, 34
savannas, 8, 30, *31*
shape, 6
size, 5
skin, 9
smell, *11*, 20
speed, *14*
survival, 36, 38–39

tail, 9
teeth, 7, 9
temporal glands, 20, 24
trunk, 11, *12*, 13, *15*
tusks, 6, *7*, 8, *39*
    for fighting, 23
    for ivory, 35, 36, (*see also* ivory
        trade)

weight, 5
wells, 32–33